Horrid Henry's
Annual 2016

Horrid Henry's Annual 2016

Francesca Simon

Illustrated by Tony Ross

Orion
Children's Books

First published in Great Britain in 2015
by Orion Children's Books
An imprint of Hachette Children's Group
Part of Hodder & Stoughton Ltd
Carmelite House
50 Victoria Embankment
London EC4Y 0DZ
An Hachette UK Company

This compilation, Horrid Henry's Annual 2016 © Orion Children's Books 2015
Text © Francesca Simon 2015
Illustrations © Tony Ross 2015

Compiled by Sally Byford from the Horrid Henry books by Francesca Simon
& illustrated by Tony Ross

The rights of Francesca Simon to be identified as the author and of Tony Ross to be identified as the illustrator of this work have been asserted by them in accordance with the Copyright, Designs and Patents Act, 1988.

A CIP catalogue record for this book is available from the British Library.

ISBN 978 1 4440 1526 3

2 4 6 8 10 9 7 5 3 1

Printed and bound in Germany

www.orionchildrensbooks.co.uk
www.horridhenry.co.uk

Contents

1

HELLO, FANS!

Get ready for another action-packed year!

This is the year when ALL my evil enemies bite the dust. The year when they ALL have to bow before King Henry the Horrible. The year when they beg to join my Purple Hand Gang. (Dream on, fools!)

If it's half as good as last year, when I proved once and for all I was the king of cakes, played my best-ever trick on Peter, and wrote loads of extra advice on how to tame your parents and annoying brothers and sisters, it will be my most horrid year ever.

Henry

Spot the Splodges

Henry has squirted splodges of Krazy Ketchup throughout this Annual. How many can you find?

Horrid Henry's New Year Plans to Defeat his Evil Enemies

1. Knock Moody Margaret's cake out of the bake-off competition.

2. Keep Peter under control with a load of new tricks, including some top secret magic.

3. Moody Margaret – watch out! I know all your Secret Club codes. I'll be pouncing when you least expect me. Your club is DOOMED.

4. Bossy Bill, beware! I've printed a t-shirt with that photocopy of your bottom. I'm wearing it next time Dad brings me to work with him.

5. Miss Battle-Axe will never give homework again after I've scientifically proved that homework harms children and that watching TV cures everything.

6. Stuck-Up Steve won't be bothering me again after I whisper the words 'Paintballing in Bunny Pyjamas' to him. Tee hee.

Horrid Henry's New Year's Krazy Quiz

Horrid Henry's New Year's resolution is to eat his favourite food – Krazy Ketchup – every day. Try this quiz to see how much Ketchup *you* could win.

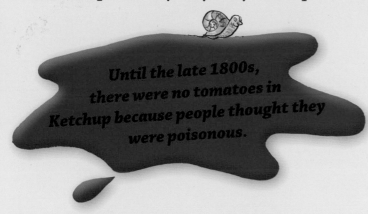

Until the late 1800s, there were no tomatoes in Ketchup because people thought they were poisonous.

1. When Henry is a billionaire, he's going to have his own brand of super tasty Ketchup

What does he plan to call it?

   a. Henry's Incredible Ketchup
   b. Henry's Healthy Ketchup
   c. Henry's Horrible Ketchup

2. Henry loves drowning his food in Krazy Ketchup.

How do his parents stop him?

   a. They hide the Ketchup
   b. They refuse to buy any Ketchup
   c. They don't let Henry squirt his own Ketchup – they do it for him

3. One Christmas at Henry's house, the lunch is a disaster.

What do they eat instead?

   a. Fish fingers
   b. Pizzas
   c. Chips and Krazy Ketchup

4. Moody Margaret is a fussy eater. She'll only eat her food if …

   a. The meat and vegetables aren't touching
   b. Everything is covered in Krazy Ketchup
   c. It's all cut up into tiny pieces

Ketchup glugs out of a glass bottle at the same speed as a snail moves – very slowly!

5. One of Henry's favourite restaurants is Gobble and Go, with its huge pizzas and lakes of ketchup.

What is its motto?

a. Krazy Ketchup for king!
b. Cucumbers are cool!
c. The chips just keep on coming!

6. Henry loves fast food, but at Restaurant Le Posh, he finds a new favourite – and he even eats it without Ketchup!

What is it?

a. Squid
b. Snails
c. Scallops

7. Henry's parents take him to Gobble and Go for a treat, but they don't eat there.

Do you know why?

a. Gobble and Go has closed – it's now the Virtuous Veggie!
b. They've run out of Krazy Ketchup – and Henry is too angry to eat
c. Henry suddenly decides to be a vegetarian

8. What is Henry horrified to discover about Ketchup?

a. That it's full of sugar
b. That it's full of salt
c. That it's full of tomatoes

If you rub a penny with Ketchup – it makes it shine!

Check out the answers on page 74. How many did you score?

6 8 SPLAT	**3–5 PLOP**	**1–2 OOZE**
Congratulations! You've earned a great big sea of yummy Krazy Ketchup. You're even allowed to splat it ALL OVER EVERYTHING ALL BY YOURSELF!	You've won a tasty plop of Krazy Ketchup, but you're not quite ready to take control of the ketchup bottle yet – so that's all you're getting!	It's just a small and slimy ooze of Vegchup for you. Brown, healthy and filled full of vegetables – this is the Ketchup Henry hates most of all in the world!

Spot the Difference

Can you circle the 6 differences between the two pictures of Henry's enemies locked up in a cage?

Evil Enemies Wordsearch

Can you find the names of some of Henry's most evil enemies in the wordsearch? Look forwards, backwards, up, down and diagonally.

CLUE
You are only looking for the names in CAPITALS.

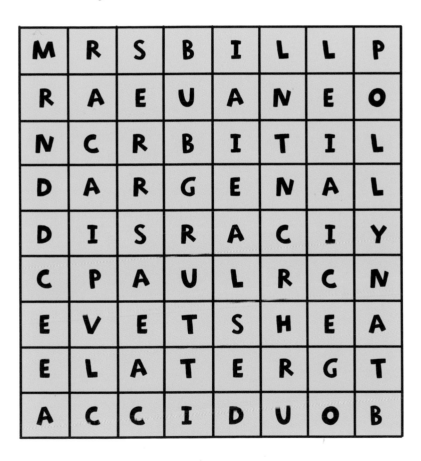

M	R	S	B	I	L	L	P
R	A	E	U	A	N	E	O
N	C	R	B	I	T	I	L
D	A	R	G	E	N	A	L
D	I	S	R	A	C	I	Y
C	P	A	U	L	R	C	N
E	V	E	T	S	H	E	A
E	L	A	T	E	R	G	T
A	C	C	I	D	U	O	B

Moody MARGARET

Perfect PETER

Sour SUSAN

Stuck-up STEVE

Bossy BILL

Prissy POLLY

Pimply PAUL

Rabid REBECCA

Miss BOUDICCA Battle-Axe

Soggy SID

Greasy GRETA

NINIUS Nerdon

Henry's newest enemy is hidden in the wordsearch.
Fill in the leftover letters in the space below to discover who it is.

_ _ _ _   _ _ _ _ _ _ _

Horrid Henry and the Revenge of the Bogey Babysitter

"When you said you were having a babysitter, you never said it could be – Rebecca," hissed Horrid Henry.

"I didn't know," whimpered Rude Ralph.

"Where's the food?" bellowed Rabid Rebecca.

Ralph's mum pointed to the kitchen. "The boys can have a small slice of cake each," she trilled. "Be good," she shouted over her shoulder as she escaped.

Then Rebecca saw Henry.

Henry saw Rebecca.

"You," said Rabid Rebecca. Her evil eyes narrowed.

"Me," said Horrid Henry.

Last time he'd met Rabid Rebecca they'd had a fight almost to the death. Henry had hoped never to have a re-match. Then he remembered her weakness …

"Don't worry, she's scared of spiders," whispered Henry.

"All we have to do is find some— "

"And don't get any ideas about spiders," said Rebecca. "I brought my friend Rachel. Nothing scares her."

Horrid Henry gasped as a terrifying fiend cast a black shadow over the sitting room.

Rancid Rachel was even tougher looking than Rabid Rebecca.

Rancid Rachel glared at Henry and Ralph. Her fangs gleamed.

"If I were you, I'd get straight to bed," growled Rachel. "That way I won't step on you by mistake."

"But what about my chocolate cake?" squeaked Ralph. "My mum said—"

"Our cake, you mean," said the bogey babysitters.

"Don't you touch that cake!"squeaked Ralph.

"Yeah," said Horrid Henry. "Or else."

Rancid Rachel cracked her knuckles.

"Or else what?" she snarled.

Horrid Henry took a step back.

"Ooh, doesn't that cake look yummy," said Rachel. "Doncha think, Becs?"

"Yeah," said Rabid Rebecca. "I can't wait to eat it. Nice of the brat's mum to leave it all for us. Now go to bed before we EAT … YOU!"

"I'm not moving," said Horrid Henry.

"Yeah," said Rude Ralph. "Make me."

"GET OUT OF HERE!" boomed the bogey babysitters, exhaling their dragon breath.

Horrid Henry and Rude Ralph sat in his bedroom. They could hear the bogey babysitters cackling and laughing in the kitchen below.

"We've got to stop them stealing all the cake," said Ralph. "It's not fair."

"I know," said Henry.

"But how?" said Ralph. "She told us to stay in bed."

"So what," said Horrid Henry. He scowled. There had to be something they could do to stop the crime of the century.

"How?" said Ralph. "Call the police?"

Tempting, thought Horrid Henry. But somehow he didn't think the police would be too keen to race over and arrest two horrible babysitters for scoffing a cake.

"We could tell Rebecca it's poisoned," said Ralph.

"What, your mum made you a poisoned cake?" said Henry. "Don't think they'd believe you."

Rude Ralph hung his head.

"It's hopeless," said Ralph. "Now we won't get any."

No cake? No yummy chocolate cake dripping with fudgy frosting and studded with sweets?

Horrid Henry wasn't the Squisher of Sitters for nothing. Wasn't there some film he'd seen, or story he'd heard, where … where …

"Get some keys and some string," said Henry. "And one of your dad's suits on a hanger. Hurry."

"Why?" said Ralph.

"Do you want that cake or don't you?" said Henry. "Now do exactly what I say."

What is Henry's master plan and does it work? Find out in '**Horrid Henry and the Revenge of the Bogey Babysitter**' from *Horrid Henry's Krazy Ketchup*.

Horrid Henry's Guide to Babysitters

Want to know how to beat a bogey babysitter?
Check out Henry's Top Tips and Tactics.

Top Tips

1. Scoff all the biscuits and fizzy pop before the babysitter does.

2. If you get into a TV battle and the babysitter seems to be winning, stand, jump or dance in front of the TV.

3. Even better, turn the TV to your favourite programme before the babysitter arrives and hide the remote.

4. Make so much noise that the babysitter leaves ... and never comes back.

5. Or stay so quiet the babysitter forgets you are there – then you can stay up really late and do whatever you want.

6. Find out your babysitter's secret fear. This could come in very handy -

tee hee!

Top Tactics

Crabby Chris

She's very cross!

Try hiding her homework and pouring red grape juice down her new white jeans.

Rabid Rebecca

She's the biggest, bossiest, meanest, ugliest teenager ever. She hogs the TV and pigs out on the biscuits. She sent Rude Ralph to bed at six o'clock, made Tough Toby get into his pyjamas at five o'clock and do all his homework, and ordered Moody Margaret to wash the floor.

She has a secret fear of spiders so threatening her with one is sure to turn her into a whimpering mess!

Tetchy Tess

She's always in a bad temper!

She's hard to get rid of, so you'll need to do something REALLY bad, like flooding the bathroom.

Rancid Rachel

She's even bigger, bossier, meaner, uglier and more hideously horrible than Rabid Rebecca. And she isn't even scared of spiders.

I'll have to come up with an extra-sneaky plan to get rid of this bogey babysitter.

The Babysitter Challenge

Have you got what it takes to bulldoze a bogey babysitter?
Follow the arrows and find out!

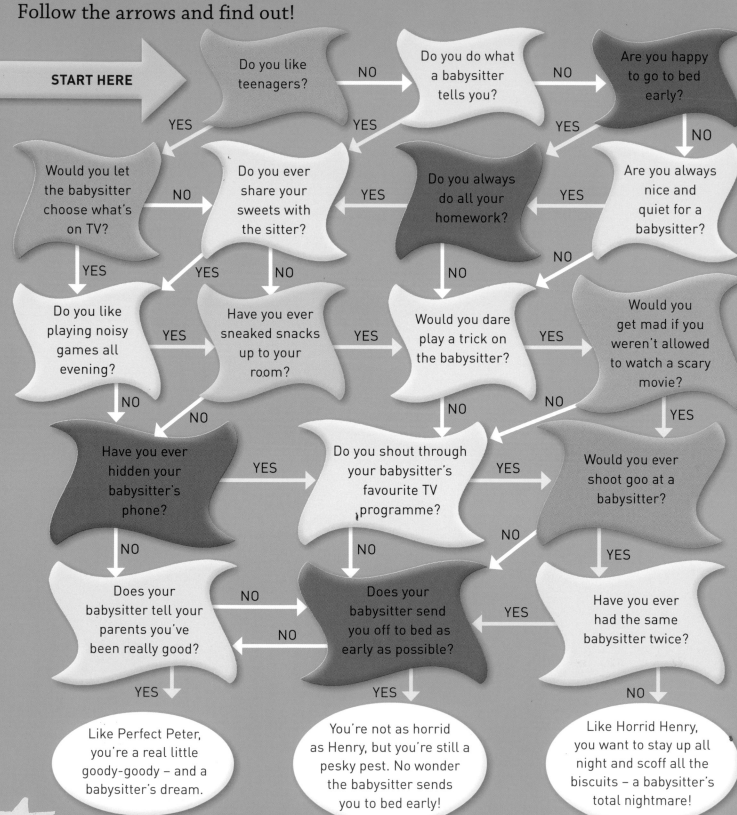

START HERE

Do you like teenagers? — **NO** → Do you do what a babysitter tells you? — **NO** → Are you happy to go to bed early?

Would you let the babysitter choose what's on TV? — **NO** → Do you ever share your sweets with the sitter? ← **YES** — Do you always do all your homework? ← **YES** — Are you always nice and quiet for a babysitter?

Do you like playing noisy games all evening? — **YES** → Have you ever sneaked snacks up to your room? — **YES** → Would you dare play a trick on the babysitter? — **YES** → Would you get mad if you weren't allowed to watch a scary movie?

Have you ever hidden your babysitter's phone? — **YES** → Do you shout through your babysitter's favourite TV programme? — **YES** → Would you ever shoot goo at a babysitter?

Does your babysitter tell your parents you've been really good? — **NO** → Does your babysitter send you off to bed as early as possible? ← **YES** — Have you ever had the same babysitter twice?

YES → Like Perfect Peter, you're a real little goody-goody – and a babysitter's dream.

YES → You're not as horrid as Henry, but you're still a pesky pest. No wonder the babysitter sends you to bed early!

NO → Like Horrid Henry, you want to stay up all night and scoff all the biscuits – a babysitter's total nightmare!

Party Pooper Crossword

Work out from the clues below who Henry doesn't want to invite to his birthday party and fill their names in the crossword below.

Across

2. This rude boy didn't invite Henry to his party.

5. This girl is very lazy.

6. Henry definitely doesn't want to invite this little worm!

Down

1. She's too moody!

3. He just cries all the time.

4. He's no fun because he's always worrying.

Dares and Double Dares

When Horrid Henry is forced to invite his enemies like Moody Margaret and Sour Susan to his birthday party, this is the perfect game to play.

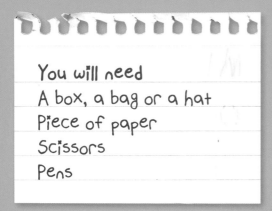

You will need
A box, a bag or a hat
Piece of paper
Scissors
Pens

DOUBLE DARE!
Let the other kids wrap you
up in loo roll like a mummy!

What to do

Cut the paper into small pieces.

On each piece, write a different dare.

To half of the dares, add the words DOUBLE DARE! Then fold up the pieces of paper, and put them in the box.

How to play

1. Sit everyone in a circle.

2. Hand the box of dares to one of the players and ask a grown-up to start the music.

3. Now pass the box of dares round the circle until the music stops.

4. The player who is holding the box when the music stops picks out a dare and has to perform it.

5. But if the player picks out a DOUBLE DARE, that player can pick a friend – or enemy – to do their dare instead.

Here are some of Henry's ideas. Beware the double dares!

DOUBLE DARE! ✗
Stand outside in the street and hold a sign, saying: I AM A WORM.

Eat a piece of birthday cake – without using your hands.

Crumple up a piece of wrapping paper using only one hand.

Eat a chocolate bar using a knife and fork.

DOUBLE DARE! ✗
Stand on one foot and sing a nursery rhyme.

DOUBLE DARE! ✗
Munch up 20 carrot sticks without being sick!

DOUBLE DARE! ✗
Rub your tummy and pat your head – at the same time.

Eat a mouthful of dry crackers, and then try to whistle.

Sneak Peter's favourite fluffy toy, Bunnykins, out of his bedroom and hide it in the fridge.

Cluck like a chicken.

DOUBLE DARE! ✗
Tell Henry's mum and dad that this is the worst party ever.

WHAT'S YOUR BEST DARE?

Easter Eggy Jokes

Match the words to these eggy jokes and complete the punchlines.
Then fit them into the criss-cross puzzle. One word has
already been filled in to help you.

2 letters	3 letters	4 letters	5 letters
UP	EGG	PONG	TABLE
			WHITE

6 letters	7 letters	8 letters	10 letters
BEATEN	MISLAID	MERINGUE	TERMINATED

1.

What happens when you play table tennis with a rotten egg?

First it goes ping, then it goes

_ _ _ _ .

2.

What happens when you tell an Easter egg a joke?

It cracks

_ _ .

3.

Why couldn't the chicken find her eggs?

They were

_ _ _ _ _ _ _ .

4.

Waiter! Waiter! This egg is bad.

Don't blame me, I only laid the

_ _ _ _ _ .

5.

Why did the Easter egg win the race?

It couldn't be

_ _ _ _ _ _ .

6.

What do you get if you cross an egg with a barrel of gunpowder?

A boom-

M E R I N G U E .

26

7.

What happens when you throw Easter eggs at a Dalek?

It's eggs-

_ _ _ _ _ _ _ _ .

8.

What happens when you take the yolk out of an egg?

It's all

_ _ _ _ _ .

9.

What did Mr and Mrs Chicken call their baby?

_ _ _ _ .

M E R I N G U E

CLUE
Fill in the 10-letter word first.

Horrid Henry's Evil Enemies Quiz

How much do you know about
Horrid Henry and his evil enemies?

1. Henry's new enemy, Rancid Rachel, is Rabid Rebecca's uglier, meaner friend. But even this tough teenager is scared of something – what is it?

a. Henry's hamster, Fang

b. Ghosts

c. Snakes

2. At Rich Aunt Ruby's, how do Stuck-up Steve and Bossy Bill try to get Henry into trouble?

a. They send him to sneak Rich Aunt Ruby's posh chocolates

b. They pick all the flowers and tell Aunt Ruby that Henry did it

c. They dare Henry to jump off the top bunk

3. What happens to Perfect Peter in the story Henry writes about him for his newspaper, *The Basher*?

a. He's thrown into the Black Lagoon

b. He's sent to prison for three years

c. He's forced to walk the plank

4. In the election for the School Council, Moody Margaret promises she'll make a great president because …?

a. She knows how to tell people what to do

b. She'll run a Gotcha club at lunchtime

c. She'll make every day a Goo-Shooter day

5. What rude name does Henry call his new teacher, Mr Ninius Nerdon?

a. Ninius Ninny
b. Nerdy Nerd
c. Ninny Noo Noo

6. When Bossy Bill tells everyone that Henry photocopied his own bottom, what nickname does Sour Susan call Henry?

a. Toad bottom!
b. Big big bottom!
c. No pants frogface!

7. What happens to Miss Battle-Axe when Henry creates chaos in the classroom on project day?

a. She screams at the class and has to go to the Head's office
b. She jumps up and down on all the projects
c. She runs from the classroom screaming

8. Greasy Greta the Demon Dinner Lady returns to school with a new job. What is it?

a. Head teacher
b. Swimming teacher
c. Healthy food monitor

Check out the answers on page 74.
How many did you score?

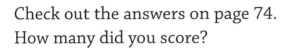

0–3 AWFUL	4–6 AVERAGE	7–8 AWESOME
Your score is as pathetic as nappypants Peter!	If Henry's evil enemy, Miss Battle-Axe, was marking your quiz, she'd definitely screech, "Try harder!"	This score is so good, you must be one of Henry's evil enemies yourself!! Watch out Henry doesn't throw you in a vat of boiling oil!

Krazy Ketchup Tricks for April Fools' Day

You will need
Clingfilm
Ketchup bottle

What to do

1. Take the lid off the ketchup, and carefully stretch a small piece of clingfilm over the top of the bottle, then put the lid back on.

2. When your victim tries again and again to squirt a big dollop of ketchup on their plate, nothing will come out!

You will need
An unripe banana
(with a hard skin)
A knife
Ketchup
A teaspoon
Kitchen paper or tissues

What to do

1. Carefully cut along the length of the banana, then use a teaspoon to scoop out the fruit.

2. Squirt ketchup into the empty banana skin, then smooth down the skin so no one can tell it's full of ketchup.

3. Offer your victim the banana and watch as they try to eat it!

KK

HENRY'S TOP TIP!
Don't do this trick inside your house, or your parents will stop your pocket money for a whole year!

Perfect Peter's Pencil and Paper Page

You have witnessed a terrible crime and the police have asked for a description so they can draw a picture of the criminal's face. Take it in turns to be the witness or the police detective and find out if you could catch the criminal.

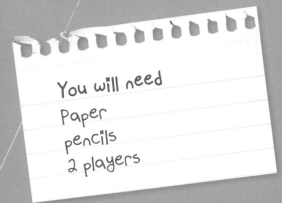

You will need
Paper
pencils
2 players

How to play

1. Sit everyone in a circle.

2. The witness decides who the criminal is, but doesn't tell the other player.

3. The witness then describes the criminal to the detective, using six different characteristics of the criminal's face:

a. Shape of face
b. Hair
c. Eyes
d. Nose
e. Mouth
f. Extras – like glasses, beard, moustache, earrings

4. The detective draws a picture of the criminal, and then guesses who it is.

5. If you have more than 2 players, one person is the witness and all the others are detectives and do their own drawings.

Try drawing a picture here from the description below:

Shape of face Long and thin with a pointy chin

Hair Grey and straggly, with a fringe

Eyes Small, black and beady

Nose Long and pointed

Mouth Thin lips, usually frowning

Extras Glasses perched on end of nose

Horrid Henry's Purple Hand Holiday Game

Take it in turns to throw the die and draw a skull and crossbones flag.
Whose flag will be finished first?

> You will need
> Two or more players
> A die
> Paper and pencil for
> each player

How to play

1. Give each player a pencil and a piece of paper. Each player must draw their own skull and crossbones flag.

2. Take it in turns to throw the die. Throw a 6 first to draw your flag.

3. Next, throw a 5 to draw a skull on your flag.

4. To complete your flag, you need to throw a 4 to draw on an eye (there are two eyes so you'll need to do this twice), a 3 for the nose, a 2 for the mouth and a 1 for a crossbone (twice). You can draw these in any order – for example, if you get a 1 at your second go, you can add on one of the crossbones straight away.

5. The first player to complete their skull and crossbones flag is the WINNER.

Throw a 6 and draw the flag.

Next, throw a 5 for the skull.

You need two 4s for the eyes.

3 for the nose.

2 for the mouth.

Two 1s for the crossbones.

Top Travel Agent

Holidays. It's so important to match the person and the place.
Here's where I'd like to send all my evil enemies on a one-way ticket.

1. Stuck-up Steve

Steve is the world's biggest scaredy-cat.
I'm sure spending two weeks alone in
the world's most haunted house would
be the holiday of a lifetime.

2. Perfect Peter

Making him a regular on the TV
show Gross-Out, where Marvin the
Maniac would fire Goo-Shooters at
him non-stop.

3. Moody Margaret

Activity holiday swimming with
sharks. No cage required.

4. Miss Battle-Axe

Miss Battle-Axe loves history. Where better than giving her a taste of Ancient Rome?

Experience life as a Roman galley slave! You'll be rowing 24/7 for the rest of your days.

5. Bossy Bill

Bill loves bossing people around. Let's see how he does with animals. Bossy Bill, your snake-pit in the desert awaits.

7. Rabid Rebecca

The Amazonian jungle, the most spider-infested place on earth! Home of the Brazilian Wandering Spider, the world's deadliest. Parachute her in.

6. Greasy Greta
the Demon Dinner Lady

I know Greasy Greta would enjoy a month long FAST at a health spa where all you get to eat is seaweed. Yum.

Horrid Henry and the Secret Club

"NUNGA!!!" screeched Henry again. "You have to let me in! I know the password."

"What do we do?" hissed Susan. "You said anyone who knows the password enters."

"For the last time, NUNGAAAAA!" shouted Horrid Henry.

"Nunga Nu," said Margaret. "Enter."

Henry swaggered into the tent. Margaret glared at him.

"Don't mind if I do," said Henry, grabbing all the chocolate biscuits and stuffing them into his mouth. Then he sprawled on the rug, scattering crumbs everywhere.

"What are you doing?" said Horrid Henry.

"Nothing," said Moody Margaret.

"Nothing," said Sour Susan.

"You are, too," said Henry.

"Mind your own business," said Margaret. "Now Susan, let's vote on whether to allow boys in. I vote No."

"I vote No, too," said Susan.

"Sorry, Henry, you can't join. Now leave."

"No," said Henry.

"LEAVE," said Margaret.

"Make me," said Henry.

Margaret took a deep breath. Then she opened her mouth and screamed. No one could scream as loud, or as long, or as piercingly, as Moody Margaret. After a few moments, Susan started screaming too.

Henry got to his feet, knocking over the crate they used as a table.

"Watch out," said Henry. "Because the Purple Hand will be back!" He turned to go.

Moody Margaret sprang up behind him and pushed him through the flap. Henry landed in a heap outside.

"Can't get me!" shouted Henry. He picked himself up and jumped over the wall. "The Purple Hand is the best!"

"Oh yeah," muttered Margaret. "We'll see about that."

Does the Purple Hand or the Secret Club come out on top? Find out in **'Horrid Henry and the Secret Club'** from *Horrid Henry and the Secret Club*.

Moody Margaret Wordsearch

Can you find all the Moody Margaret words
in the puzzle below?

T	Y	S	S	O	R	C	E	F	N
R	P	A	E	M	Y	C	L	O	I
U	M	H	I	C	A	T	T	O	A
M	U	C	L	F	R	D	E	T	T
P	R	T	G	M	A	E	A	B	P
E	G	O	G	G	I	T	A	A	A
T	R	G	G	E	M	U	F	L	C
F	S	E	T	A	R	I	P	L	F
I	R	Y	H	C	U	O	R	G	N
S	T	O	O	B	Y	S	S	O	B

FOOTBALL

GRUMPY

CROSS

PIRATES

BOSSYBOOTS

TRUMPET

GOTCHA

SECRET

CAPTAIN

GROUCHY

DAGGER

FROGFACE

The leftover letters reveal what Margaret's mum calls her!

-- ------- -----

Bubble Trouble

It's the summer holidays, and the Purple Hand and the Secret Club are battling – with bubbles.

To make the bubble mixture

Half a cup of washing-up liquid

2 cups of water

1 tablespoon glycerine (this is great for making the big bubbles, but it isn't essential)

An empty plastic bottle

These things are also useful

Plastic containers

Washing-up bowl

Drinking straws

How to do it

1. Mix the washing-up liquid with the water in the plastic bottle. If you've got the glycerine, add that too.

2. Don't shake the bottle or the mixture will be too bubbly before you've even started!

3. Ask an adult to make bubble wands for you out of garden wire, pipe cleaners, or to blow really big bubbles, out of wire coat hangers.

How to make bubble wands – adults only!

You will need
garden wire or pipe cleaners
wire coat hanger, wire cutters
a straight stick, duct tape,
string

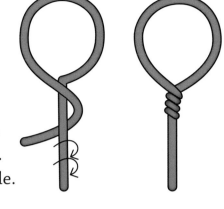

To make a small wand, using garden wire or a pipe cleaner: Bend the wire in half, and form a circle where the wire bends. Twist the ends of the wire to form the handle. Cover any sharp ends with duct tape.

To make a large wand, using a coat hanger: Twist the hanging section into a big circle. Cut off the hooked end using the wire cutters. Fasten the stick to the twisted section of the hanger using duct tape to create a handle and to cover any sharp ends, and wrap string around it until it's secure.

Bubble Games

Bubble Bursting

Take it in turns to blow hundreds of tiny bubbles using the drinking straws and time how long it takes your rivals to burst them all.

Bubble Balancing

Using small bubble wands, blow perfect bubbles, then try to catch and balance them on your wands. The first gang to catch 10 bubbles is the winner.

Biggest Bubbles

Pour the bubble mixture into a washing-up bowl, then dip in your biggest bubble wands. The gang that can blow the biggest bubble is the winner.

39

Keeping Secrets from the Enemy

TOP SECRET

The Purple Hand Gang

Invisible Ink

Henry's mum is delighted when Henry asks for a drink of milk. But Henry isn't planning to drink it. Instead he dips a paintbrush into the milk and uses it to write a secret message to Ralph! The milk dries invisible. To read the message, Ralph holds the paper near the warmth from a radiator – and Henry's message soon mysteriously reappears.

RALPH

MEET IN THE FORT AFTER TEA.

WE HAVE TO MAKE TOP SECRET PLANS.

HENRY

Purple Hand Language

Whenever Perfect Peter hangs around, or Sour Susan is trying to sneak the Purple Hand secrets, Henry and Ralph speak their own special language! They add 'ugg' before the first vowel (that's a, e, i, o and u) in a word. So Henry is called Huggenry and Ralph is called Ruggalph.

Can you work out what they are saying to each other?

Ralph: Whuggat uggis thugge Puggurple Huggand cuggode cruggacker luggetter?

Henry: Uggit uggis thugge fuggirst luggetter uggof yuggour luggeader's nuggame.

Purple Hand Secret Code

It's time to plan a raid on the Secret Club – and Henry and Ralph communicate in code. Their code gives each letter a number, but instead of starting with A as 1, there's a code cracker letter – '**h**' – which means that **h=1**, as shown below.

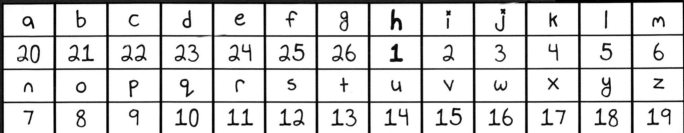

a	b	c	d	e	f	g	**h**	i	j	k	l	m
20	21	22	23	24	25	26	**1**	2	3	4	5	6
n	o	p	q	r	s	t	u	v	w	x	y	z
7	8	9	10	11	12	13	14	15	16	17	18	19

Can you de-code Henry and Ralph's messages and work out what they are planning to do?

12-13-2-7-4-21-8-6-21
20-13-13-20-22-4
8-7   12-24-22-11-24-13
22-5-14-21
13-8-7-2-26-1-13.

1-24-7-11-18

Henry's code to Ralph says:

26-11-24-24-13-2-7-26-12
5-24-20-23-24-11

23-24-20-23   25-2-12-1
20-7-23
11-8-13-13-24-7
24-26-26-12   8-4 ?

11-20-5-9-1

Ralph's secret reply says:

The Secret Club

Moody Margaret and Sour Susan
are swapping their own plans to get
revenge on the Purple Hand.

No Ink Invisible Messages

Margaret writes a secret message to
Susan without using any special ink. She
takes two sheets of paper, and puts one
on top of the other. Then she writes her
message on the top paper, pressing hard.
She removes the top piece of paper and
tears it up. To read the message, Susan
gently shades over it with a pencil – and
the message magically appears.

Nunga Nu!

Top Secret Plans to
destroy the Purple Hand
Gang, once and for all!
Prepare your spy report
and await a secret
code message from your
leader. The secret letter
for the code is 'm'.

The Secret Club Code

Margaret makes sure that Henry can't crack the Secret Club code.
See if you can crack it!

A secret letter is inserted at the end of each word – Margaret has chosen 'm'. So if
she wants to write to Susan: **Linda is chief spy now not you**, it looks like this:

Lindam ism chiefm spym nowm notm youm.

Then she turns it into one long word.

Lindamismchiefmspymnowmnotmyoum.

And finally breaks it up into three letter words:

Lin dam ism chi efm spy mno wmn otm you m.

Can you crack Margaret and Susan's messages?

Wem str ike mto day man dms wap mth emP urp lem Han dmG ang mfi zzy wiz zmw ith mDu nge onm Dri nkm.

Bem the rem orm Imw ill mas kmG uri nde rmi nst ead mof myo um.

Why mam mIm fri end smw ith mam mea nmm ood ymb oss ybo ots mli kem youm?

Dom itm you rse lfm.

Imq uit m!

Can you put the message below into the Purple Hand Secret Code?

WATCH OUT!

THE PURPLE HAND WILL BE BACK!

ACID

DUNGEON DRINK

Recipes

BANG POO

Margaret's code note to Susan says:

Susan's code note to Margaret says:

Write your code message here:

43

Chief Spy Treasure Hunt Maze

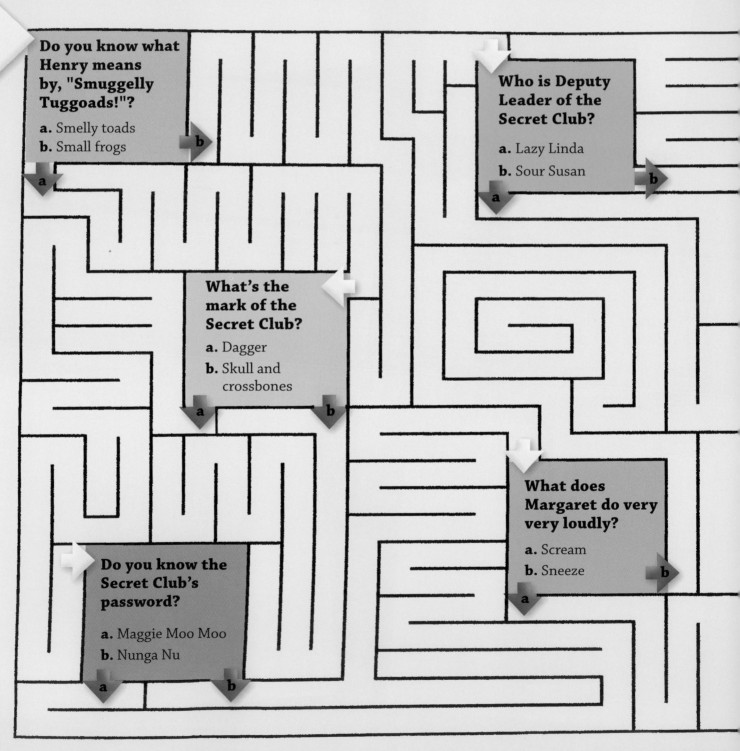

Do you know what Henry means by, "Smuggelly Tuggoads!"?
a. Smelly toads
b. Small frogs

Who is Deputy Leader of the Secret Club?
a. Lazy Linda
b. Sour Susan

What's the mark of the Secret Club?
a. Dagger
b. Skull and crossbones

What does Margaret do very very loudly?
a. Scream
b. Sneeze

Do you know the Secret Club's password?
a. Maggie Moo Moo
b. Nunga Nu

Horrid Henry, Leader of the Purple Hand Gang, makes you Chief Spy and sends you off to sneak treasure from his rivals, the Secret Club.

If you get the right answer to each clue, you'll find your way to the next clue. But if you get the wrong answer – you'll hit a dead end, and you'll have to retrace your steps!

Start at the big arrow on page 44.

Where do the Secret Club keep their cookies?

a. In a tin under a blanket

a **b.** In a school bag **b**

What is the Secret Club den?

a. Garden shed

b. Tent

a **b**

Can you crack Margaret's note to Susan?

Mee tmi nmt hme den mat msi xm

a. Me and Linda are best friends

b. Meet in the den at six

a **b**

Can you crack Henry's note?

13-2-6-24 13-8
12-7-24-20-4 13-1-24
22-8-8-4-2-24-12!

a. Time to sneak the cookies!

b. Look out, it's Margaret **b**

a

Well done, Chief Spy!

Master Spy Fingerprint Kit

Everyone's fingerprints are different, so testing for prints is a great way to find out if your enemies have been sneaking your glass of fizzywizz or pinching your biscuits.

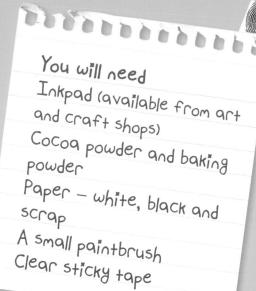

You will need
Inkpad (available from art and craft shops)
Cocoa powder and baking powder
Paper – white, black and scrap
A small paintbrush
Clear sticky tape

What to do

If you are testing a glass for prints, brush cocoa powder onto the surface, using the paintbrush.

Press the sticky tape over any fingerprints you find, then gently pull the tape off the glass, and stick the prints to your white paper.

If you are testing something dark, like a black or purple tin, brush the surface with baking powder and tape your prints to the black paper.

How to take an enemy's fingerprints

Ask your enemy to press their fingers onto your ink pad. Then first press their fingers onto a piece of scrap paper so that they aren't too inky, then on a spy record – like the one below.

All you need to do now is to see if they are the same fingerprints that you found on your glass or tin! If they match, you've found your sneaky thief!

Practise with your own fingerprints first on this spy record

SPY RECORD: FINGERPRINTS BELONGING TO:					
LEFT HAND					
RIGHT HAND					

Greedy Gruham's Munchy Mug Grub

You will need
25g of self-raising flour
35g of sugar
1 tablespoon of cocoa
A tiny pinch of salt
A tiny pinch of cinnamon
2 small drops of vanilla essence
2 tablespoons of water
1 tablespoon of vegetable oil
A microwave-safe mug
Ice cream, to serve

Top Tip For Master Spies!

Anyone who eats this cake will have the stickiest fingers ever – perfect for fingerprints!

What to do

1. Put the flour, sugar, cocoa, salt and cinnamon in the mug and stir everything together with a teaspoon.

2. Add the water, oil and vanilla essence, then stir again, making sure there aren't any lumps or little pockets of flour.

3. Ask a grown-up to put the mug in the microwave. Cook your cake for 60 seconds on the highest power level,

then have a look at it. If the cake is still runny in the middle, cook for another 30 seconds.

4. When the cake comes out of the microwave, it will be VERY HOT so let it cool for a few minutes before you taste. It's even more delicious with a scoop of ice cream on top.

Horrid Henry's Arch Enemy

"I'm going to tell my dad that you attacked me," said Bill. "In fact, I'm going to tell my dad every single bad thing you do in school. Then he'll tell yours and you'll get into trouble. And won't I laugh."

Henry's blood boiled. What had he ever done to deserve Bossy Bill butting into his life? A spy in his class. Could school get any worse?

Aerobic Al jogged past.

"Henry photocopied his bottom at my dad's office," said Bill loudly. "Boy, did he get into trouble."

AAARRRGGHHH!

"That's a lie," said Horrid Henry hotly. "Bill did, not me."

"Yeah right, Henry," said Dizzy Dave.

"Big bottom!" shrieked Moody Margaret.

"Big big bottom!" shrieked Sour Susan.

Bill smirked.

"Bye, big bottom," said Bill. "Don't forget, I'm watching you," he hissed.

Henry sat down by himself on the broken bench in the secret garden. He had to get Bill out of his class. School was horrible enough without someone evil like Bill spying on him and spreading foul rumours. His life would be ruined. He had to get rid of Bill – fast. But how?

Maybe he could get Bill to run screaming from school and never come back. Wow, thought Horrid Henry. Wouldn't that be wonderful? Bye bye Bossy Bill.

Or maybe he could get Bill to photocopy his bottom again. Probably not, thought Horrid Henry regretfully. Aha! He could trick Bill into dancing nude on Miss Battle-Axe's desk singing "I'm a busy bumblebee – buzz buzz buzz." That would be sure to get him expelled. The only trouble was – how?

I've got to think of something, thought Horrid Henry desperately. I've just got to.

Does Henry think up a plan to get Bossy Bill out of his school? Find out in **'Horrid Henry's Arch Enemy'** from *Horrid Henry and the Football Fiend.*

Nasty Names Criss Cross

Horrid Henry calls Perfect Peter lots of nasty names.
Can you fit them into the puzzle below?

4 Letters
TOAD
UGLY
WORM

5 Letters
POOPY
NAPPY

6 Letters
SMELLY
STINKY

7 Letters
CRYBABY

8 Letters
TELLTALE
FROGFACE

10 Letters
PONGYPANTS

CLUE
Fill in the 10-letter word first.

Enemy Spotting at School

There are lots of Henry's enemies in the playground. Can you spot 10 of them?

1 _____

2 _____

3 _____

4 _____

5 _____

6 _____

7 _____

8 _____

9 _____

10 _____

Which Enemy Are You?

If you were one of Horrid Henry's enemies, which one would you be?
Try this quiz and find out.

1. Describe yourself in two words:

a. Brilliant and beautiful
b. Brainy and brave
c. Kind and clever
d. Happy and helpful
e. Funny and friendly

2. My favourite colour is?

a. Green
b. Blue
c. Pink
d. Black
e. Red

3. Which of these animals do you like best?

a. Hedgehog
b. Weasel
c. Rabbit
d. Shark
e. Rat

4. What do you want to do when you grow up?

a. Become Prime Minister
b. Be the boss of a big business
c. Take care of sick animals
d. Babysit – you'd get paid loads for watching TV
e. I'll be so rich I won't have to do anything

5. What makes you happy?

a. Getting my own way
b. Laughing at other people
c. Helping others
d. Scaring others
e. Money

6. What makes you angry?

a. People who won't do as they are told
b. Getting into trouble
c. Horrid big brothers
d. Noisy little kids
e. Not getting enough Christmas presents

7. What do you like doing with your friends?

a. Bossing them about
b. Playing tricks on them
c. Doing good deeds together
d. Pushing little kids around
e. Showing off all my new toys

8. Which of these statements best describes you?

a. I always win at everything
b. I have better ideas than anyone else
c. I am always the top of the class
d. NOBODY dares get cross with me
e. I deserve to have the best of everything

So, which evil enemy are you?

Mostly (a)s:	Mostly (b)s:	Mostly (c)s:	Mostly (d)s:	Mostly (e)s:
You're Moody Margaret	**You're Bossy Bill**	**You're Perfect Peter**	**You're Rabid Rebecca**	**You're Stuck-up Steve**
Grumpy, mean and competitive – you're only happy when you're the boss.	Sneaky and sly, you are a big troublemaker, but you hate it when things backfire and you end up in bother.	Well-behaved and keen to please, you're the teacher's pet but you can be a bit of a sneaky tell-tale.	Tough and terrifying, no one ever dares to mess with you.	Spoiled and whiny, you get everything you want, and think you're better than everyone else.

the Healthy Food Hoax

One of Henry's classmates is playing tricks on him.
Can you solve the puzzles and help Henry work out the mystery?

School Fair Trick

Miss Battle-Axe announces that everyone has to help
at the Autumn School Fair. She puts a list of stalls on
the noticeboard so pupils can write their names against
their chosen stall. But when Henry looks, he's too late.
One of his classmates has added his name to help on the
worst stall ever – the Healthy Fruit and Vegetable Stall!

Can you un-muddle the other six muddled-up
names and write the names in the empty boxes to
find Henry's SIX SUSPECTS.

HEALTHY FRUIT & VEGETABLE STALL	HENRY	
CAKES AND COOKIES	MARGAH	
POPPING POPCORN	SHOJ	
TOMBOLA	TRAGAMER	
COUNT THE SWEETS IN THE JAR	NASSU	
TREASURE MAP COMPETITION	RIBNA	
GOAL SHOOTING	LA	

Smiley Apple Trick

When Henry returns to his desk, someone has put an apple on his chair. Find a path for each of the suspects through the maze, past Henry's seat and to their seat at the classroom table. Only one of the six suspects doesn't pass Henry's seat – who is it?

Cross this classmate off your list of suspects. Then turn the page to continue solving the clues in the Healthy Food Hoax ...

Lunchbox Trick

It's lunchtime and Henry runs to get his Mutant Max lunchbox. Today, as a special treat, he has a bag of Pickled Onion Crisps AND a chocolate bar. But when Henry opens his lunchbox, he can't believe it!

Egg sandwiches, carrot sticks and grapes – blecccch! He's been tricked again! His final five suspects all have EXACTLY THE SAME LUNCHBOX AS HIM. One of them must have swapped it.

But who?

The lunchboxes below all look the same, but one has a small difference – so the owner of that lunchbox can be crossed off the suspect list. Can you spot the odd one out?

Horrid Henry

Moody Margaret

Jolly Josh

Brainy Brian

Sour Susan

Aerobic Al

Answer: _____

Cross this classmate off your list of suspects. Now you're down to four!

Blackboard Trick

Back in the classroom, Henry is furious when he sees that someone has written on the blackboard: HA HA, HENRY! YOU'VE BEEN TRICKED!!

Fill in the names of your final four suspects and follow the tangled strings to find out which classmate's string leads to the chalk.

Who is the class joker who has been tricking Horrid Henry all day?

Answer: _____

Horrid Henry and the Mega-Mean Time Machine

Perfect Peter walked a few steps towards the time machine. Then he paused.

"What's it like in the future?"

"Boys wear dresses," said Horrid Henry. "And lipstick. People talk Ugg language. You'd probably like it. Everyone just eats vegetables."

"Really?"

"And kids have loads of homework."

Perfect Peter loved homework.

"Ooohh." This Peter had to see. Just in case Henry was telling the truth.

"I'm going to the future and you can't stop me," said Peter.

"Go ahead," said Henry. Then he snorted. "You can't go looking like that!"

"Why not?" said Peter.

"Cause everyone will laugh at you."

Perfect Peter hated people laughing at him.

"Why?"

"Because to them you'll look weird. Are you sure you really want to go to the future?"

"Yes," said Peter.

"Are you sure you're sure?"

"YES," said Peter.

"Then I'll get you ready," said Henry solemnly.

"Thank you, Henry," said Peter. Maybe he'd been wrong about Henry. Maybe going to the future had turned him into a nice brother.

Horrid Henry dashed out of the sitting room.

Perfect Peter felt a quiver of excitement. The future. What if Henry really was telling the truth?

What does Perfect Peter discover when he travels in the Time Machine? Find out in '**Horrid Henry and the Mega-Mean Time Machine**' from *Horrid Henry and the Mega-Mean Time Machine*.

58

Horrid Henry's Top Tricks on Perfect Peter

Henry thinks the Mega-Mean Time Machine is the greatest trick he's ever played on Perfect Peter. But what are his other favourites?

Blood Boil Bob

Remember when I told Peter that Blood Boil Bob the pirate cannibal would curse him and turn him into a shrunken head if he had a pirate party? He didn't believe me – until he and his little friends were hunting for the chocolate treasure and I hid in my pirate costume. They thought I was Blood Boil Bob and ran screaming back to Mum and Dad – leaving me to scoff all the chocolates. HA HAAARRR!

Horrible Homework

Peter wrote an essay on the computer called Why I Love My Teacher – bleccch! I changed it without him knowing to Why I Hate My Teacher and made it really funny and rude. Miss Lovely was so cross she sent Peter to the Head. No Good as Gold Stars for Peter that week!

Midnight Fairies

What about the time I told Peter there were fairies at the bottom of our garden that could only be seen midnight? We sneaked out at night, and I crept off and left him stuck up a tree. When Mum and Dad discovered Peter wasn't in bed, he was in BIG trouble.

Can you describe the best trick you've ever played on your annoying little brother or sister?

Scaring Away the Enemy

On Hallowe'en, Henry scares away his enemies with some spooky door and window decorations.

Mega Monsters

Here's how to turn the whole of your front door into a giant monster face.

You will need
Coloured cardboard or paper
Sticky tape
Scissors
Paper plates
Felt pens or paints
Crepe paper or tissue paper
Masking tape

What to do

1. Have a look at your front door and plan out your monster face. A letterbox makes a great mouth, and a door knocker can be used as a nose.

2. Use the paper plates to give your monster big staring eyes. Draw or paint on the pupils. Add some angry eyebrows using masking tape, or by cutting them out of cardboard or paper.

3. Make messy monster hair out of crepe paper or tissue paper.

4. Cut scary teeth out of cardboard or paper and tape them to the door.

Spooky Window Silhouettes

Use black card or paper to create spooky silhouettes.

You will need
White paper
Pencil
Black card or paper
Scissors
Sticky tape

What to do

1. Draw the shape of your silhouette on white paper.

2. Tape your drawing on top of the black card or paper and cut out your silhouette.

3. Stick the silhouette to your window. When night falls, turn on the lights and your spooky silhouette will stand out against a glowing background.

4. How about some bats flitting across your window? Or some spiders to keep Rabid Rebecca away? Or an evil grinning pumpkin head? Or cut out letters to give your enemies a chilling warning -

ENTER IF YOU DARE

Evil Enemy Silhouettes

It's Hallowe'en, and Horrid Henry is Trick or Treating. As he sneaks up a garden path, he can see a scary silhouette in the window. Can you recognise Henry's enemies from these shadowy shapes?

E

F

G

Write your answers below:

A _____

B _____

C _____

D _____

E _____

F _____

G _____

Top Triumphs

Horrid Henry celebrates his top triumphs over his evil enemies.

1. Tricking Peter into believing that Dolores the hen laid chocolate eggs.

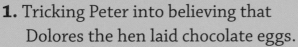

2. Terrifying both Rabid Rebecca and Rancid Rachel and nabbing all the cake for him and Ralph.

3. Scaring the Best Boys Club into giving Henry all their money by pretending there was a Fangmangler monster in the garden.

4. Telling Peter that a cardboard box was a time machine and making him think he'd travelled to the future.

5. Grabbing everyone's Hallowe'en sweets despite being stuck at home.

A Winter Wonderlund

Check out Henry's winter wonderland.
Can you spot all his friends and enemies?

christmas boxes

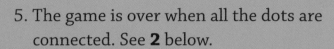

A game for two players – to play while you're waiting for your presents.

How to play

1. Draw a grid of dots, 6 dots by 6.

2. In between the dots, draw pictures of brilliant and terrible Christmas presents – like the Goo-Shooter and the socks shown below.

3. Take it in turns to draw a line between two of the dots, either horizontally or vertically.

4. When your line makes a box, write your initials in it and take another turn. See **1** below.

5. The game is over when all the dots are connected. See **2** below.

6. Count up the boxes for each player. For each box containing the good present, add on 5 points. For each box containing the bad present, take off 5 points. The player with the highest number of points is the winner.

1.

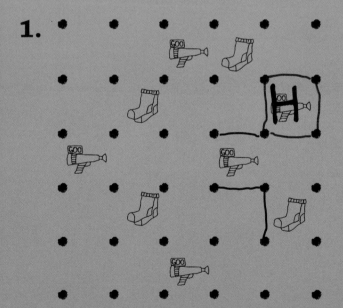

Henry is using a red pen and Peter is using a black pen. Henry has the first turn, and after four turns has already bagged himself a Goo-Shooter box. But there's still plenty of time for Peter to overtake him and win the game.

2.

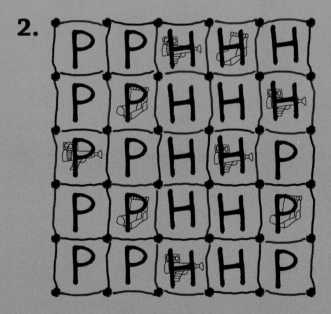

The game is over! What's the score?
Peter has 13 boxes = 13
1 Goo-Shooter ADD 5 points = 18
3 Socks TAKE AWAY 15 = **3**
Better luck next time!

Henry has 12 boxes = 12
4 Goo-Shooters ADD 20 points = 34
1 Socks TAKE AWAY 5 = **29**
Well done, Henry!

Snowy Sudoku

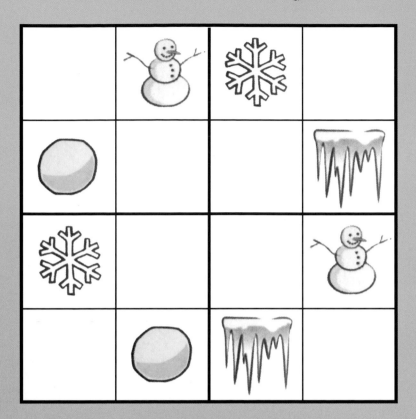

Fill in the sudoku so that every square and row – both up and down – contains these four pictures.

Too easy-peasy for you? Try a trickier one! Fill in every square and row with numbers 1–6.

CLUE
First fill in all the missing 2s, then the 3s and 6s.

		4			
			2	3	
3				6	
	6				2
5	2	1			
			5		

Horrid Henry's Christmas Quiz

	TRUE	FALSE
1. Henry's best friend is Rude Ralph	☐	☐
2. His little brother is a worm	☐	☐
3. Henry's parents have the biggest TV in the world	☐	☐
4. His favourite band is The Killer Boy Rats	☐	☐
5. Henry loves walking in the countryside	☐	☐
6. His teacher is Miss Battle-Axe	☐	☐
7. Henry's favourite school subject is swimming	☐	☐
8. His next door neighbour is Sour Susan	☐	☐
9. Henry has a pet spider called Fang	☐	☐
10. The Purple Hand Gang is the best club ever	☐	☐

This is the best Christmas Quiz ever because it's all about ME!

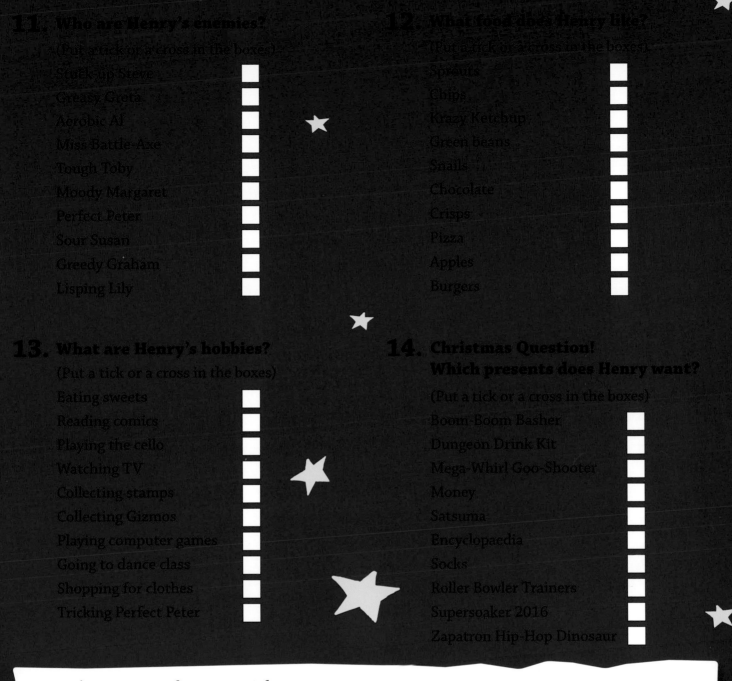

11. Who are Henry's enemies?

(Put a tick or a cross in the boxes)

Stuck-up Steve
Greasy Greta
Aerobic Al
Miss Battle-Axe
Tough Toby
Moody Margaret
Perfect Peter
Sour Susan
Greedy Graham
Lisping Lily

12. What food does Henry like?

(Put a tick or a cross in the boxes)

Sprouts
Chips
Krazy Ketchup
Green beans
Snails
Chocolate
Crisps
Pizza
Apples
Burgers

13. What are Henry's hobbies?

(Put a tick or a cross in the boxes)

Eating sweets
Reading comics
Playing the cello
Watching TV
Collecting stamps
Collecting Gizmos
Playing computer games
Going to dance class
Shopping for clothes
Tricking Perfect Peter

**14. Christmas Question!
Which presents does Henry want?**

(Put a tick or a cross in the boxes)

Boom-Boom Basher
Dungeon Drink Kit
Mega-Whirl Goo-Shooter
Money
Satsuma
Encyclopaedia
Socks
Roller Bowler Trainers
Supersoaker 2016
Zapatron Hip-Hop Dinosaur

There's one point for every right answer.
Check out your score on page 74 and read Henry's verdict below:

40+	**25 – 39**	**0 – 24**
BRILLIANT! You know LOADS about me and how FANTASTIC I am.	Miss Battle-Axe would call this mark FAIR. I call it RUBBISH!	TOTAL PANTS! Less than half marks is NOT a good score! It's time you found out a lot more about the Lord High Excellent Majesty of the Universe!

Horrid Henry's Christmas Cracker Jokes

Which Christmas carol do Henry's Mum and Dad like best?

Silent Night!

What does Miss Battle-Axe try to teach Santa's elves?

The elf-abet!

Who delivers presents to Fluffy the cat?

Santa Paws!

What do you get if you cross a bell with nappypants Perfect Peter?

Jingle Smells!

What does Greasy Greta put into her Christmas pudding?

Her teeth!

Which of Santa's reindeers is a lot like Ralph?

RUDE-olph!

STUCK-UP STEVE: I want a dog for Christmas!

RICH AUNT RUBY: Sorry darling, you're having turkey like everyone else.

Answers

Page 11

Henry has squirted 8 splodges of ketchup on pages 11, 20, 30, 34, 37, 52, 64, and 67

Pages 14-15

1. (a)	5. (c)
2. (c)	6. (b)
3. (b)	7. (a)
4. (a)	8. (c)

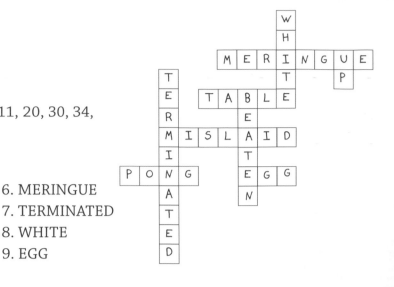

Page 17

Rancid Rachel

Page 23

Pages 26-27

1. PONG	6. MERINGUE
2. UP	7. TERMINATED
3. MISLAID	8. WHITE
4. TABLE	9. EGG
5. BEATEN	

Pages 28-29

1. (a)	5. (b)
2. (c)	6. (c)
3. (b)	7. (b)
4. (a)	8. (a)

Page 37

MY LITTLE MAGGIE MUFFIN

Pages 40-43

Henry's code to Ralph says:

Stinkbomb attack on Secret Club tonight. Henry

Ralph's secret reply says:

Greetings leader, dead fish and rotten eggs OK? Ralph

Margaret's code note to Susan says:

We strike today and I swap the Purple Hand Fizzywizz with Dungeon Drink. Be there or I will ask Gurinder instead of you.

Susan's code note to Margaret says:

Why am I friends with a mean moody bossyboots like you? Do it yourself, I quit!

The Purple Hand secret code message is:

16-20-13-22-1 8-14-13! 13-1-24 9-14-11-9-5-24 1-20-7-23 16-2-5-5 21-24 21-20-22-4!

Pages 44-45

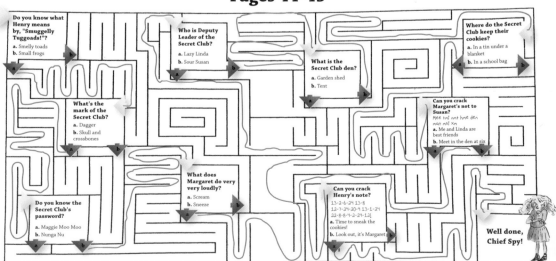

Well done, Chief Spy!

Page 49

Pages 50-51

Did you find 10 of Henry's enemies from the following?

Soggy Sid, Nitty Nora, Ninius Nerdon, Nurse Needle, Miss Impatience Tutu, Miss Battle-Axe, Perfect Peter, Moody Margaret, Sour Susan, Greasy Greta, Mrs Oddbod, Doctor Dettol, Gorgeous Gurinder, Singing Soraya, Bossy Bill, Stuck-up Steve.

Pages 54-55

GRAHAM   SUSAN
JOSH   BRIAN
MARGARET   AL

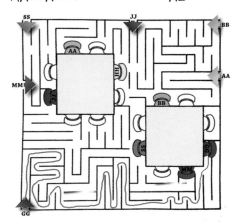

The only suspect who didn't pass Henry's seat was Greedy Graham.

Pages 56-57

The odd one out is Sour Susan

The final four suspects are:
MARGARET, AL, JOSH and BRIAN

The class joker was JOLLY JOSH

Pages 62-63

A. Miss Battle-Axe
B. Rabid Rebecca
C. Moody Margaret
D. Bossy Bill
E. Greasy Greta
F. Miss Impatience Tutu
G. Sour Susan

Page 69

2	3	4	1	5	6
1	5	6	2	3	4
3	1	2	4	6	5
4	6	5	3	1	2
5	2	1	6	4	3
6	4	3	5	2	1

Page 70-71

		TRUE	FALSE
1.	Henry's best friend is Rude Ralph	✔	
2.	His little brother is a worm	✔	
3.	Henry's parents have the biggest TV in the world		✔
4.	His favourite band is The Killer Boy Rats	✔	
5.	Henry loves walking in the countryside		✔
6.	His teacher is Miss Battle-Axe	✔	
7.	Henry's favourite school subject is swimming		✔
8.	His next door neighbour is Sour Susan		✔
9.	Henry has a pet spider called Fang		✔
10.	The Purple Hand Gang is the best club ever	✔	

11. Who are Henry's enemies?
(Put a tick or a cross in the boxes)
Stuck-up Steve	✔
Greasy Greta	✔
Aerobic Al	✘
Miss Battle-Axe	✘
Tough Toby	✘
Moody Margaret	✔
Perfect Peter	✔
Sour Susan	✔
Greedy Graham	✘
Lisping Lily	✔

12. What food does Henry like?
(Put a tick or a cross in the boxes)
Sprouts	✘
Chips	✔
Krazy Ketchup	✔
Green beans	✘
Snails	✔
Chocolate	✔
Crisps	✔
Pizza	✔
Apples	✘
Burgers	✔

13. What are Henry's hobbies?
(Put a tick or a cross in the boxes)
Eating sweets	✔
Reading comics	✔
Playing the cello	✘
Watching TV	✔
Collecting stamps	✘
Collecting Gizmos	✔
Playing computer games	✔
Going to dance class	✘
Shopping for clothes	✘
Tricking Perfect Peter	✔

14. Christmas Question! Which presents does Henry want?
(Put a tick or a cross in the boxes)
Boom-Boom Basher	✔
Dungeon Drink Kit	✔
Mega-Whirl Goo-Shooter	✔
Money	✔
Satsuma	✘
Encyclopaedia	✘
Socks	✘
Roller Bowler Trainers	✔
Supersoaker 2016	✔
Zapatron Hip-Hop Dinosaur	✔

You can read these other *Horrid Henry* titles, stories available as audio editions, read by Miranda Richardson

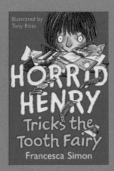

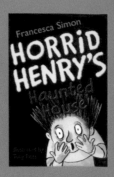

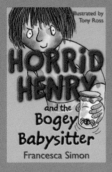

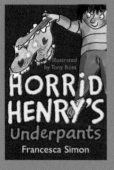

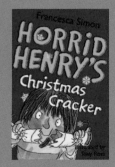
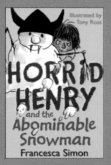

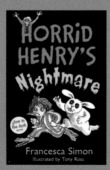

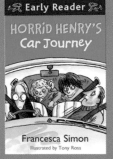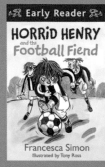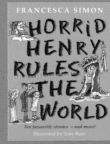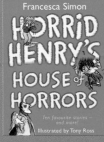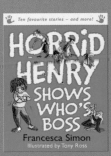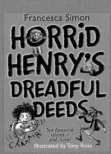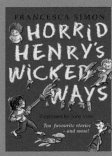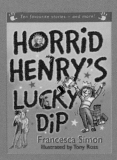